A Guide to
AMERICAN STATES

Louisiana

THE PELICAN STATE

MEDIA ENHANCED BOOKS
AV2
BY WEIGL
ADDED VALUE · AUDIO VISUAL

www.av2books.com

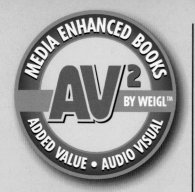

AV² provides enriched content that supplements and complements this book. Weigl's AV² books strive to create inspired learning and engage young minds in a total learning experience.

Your AV² Media Enhanced books come alive with...

Audio
Listen to sections of the book read aloud.

Key Words
Study vocabulary, and complete a matching word activity.

Go to **www.av2books.com**, and enter this book's unique code.

Video
Watch informative video clips.

Quizzes
Test your knowledge.

BOOK CODE

F 4 6 5 7 8

Embedded Weblinks
Gain additional information for research.

Slide Show
View images and captions, and prepare a presentation.

AV² by Weigl brings you media enhanced books that support active learning.

Try This!
Complete activities and hands-on experiments.

... and much, much more!

Published by AV² by Weigl
350 5th Avenue, 59th Floor
New York, NY 10118
Website: www.av2books.com   www.weigl.com

Library of Congress Cataloging-in-Publication Data

Johnstone, Robb.
 Louisiana / Robb Johnstone.
   p. cm. -- (A guide to American states)
 Includes index.
 ISBN 978-1-61690-790-7 (hardcover : alk. paper) -- ISBN 978-1-61690-466-1 (online)
 1. Louisiana--Juvenile literature. I. Title.
 F369.3.J645 2011
 976.3--dc23
                    2011018330

Printed in the United States of America in North Mankato, Minnesota

052011
WEP180511

Project Coordinator Jordan McGill
Art Director Terry Paulhus

Photo Credits
Every reasonable effort has been made to trace ownership and to obtain permission to reprint copyright material. The publishers would be pleased to have any errors or omissions brought to their attention so that they may be corrected in subsequent printings.

Weigl acknowledges Getty Images as its primary image supplier for this title.

Contents

Thousands flock to Mardi Gras celebrations across the state of Louisiana. The most popular Mardi Gras parades take place in New Orleans.

Introduction

"Let the good times roll" is a phrase sometimes shouted during Mardi Gras along the streets of New Orleans, Louisiana's most colorful city. Of course, you may also hear *"laissez les bon temps rouller,"* which means the same thing in French.

Louisiana is one of the most fascinating states in the nation. Its history links it to the French, whose influence is still highly visible. Its land is shaped by the mightiest river in North America, the Mississippi. Its people are a mix of cultures that come together every year for Mardi Gras, the biggest party in the country.

Powered by huge paddlewheels, steamboats carry tourists up and down the Mississippi River.

Louisiana music ranges from African American folk songs and rural blues to New Orleans jazz and bouncy fiddle and accordion tunes.

Louisiana has produced celebrated artists, writers, musicians, and actors. These celebrities include **jazz** musicians Louis Armstrong and Wynton Marsalis, writer Lillian Hellman, musician Fats Domino, gospel singer Mahalia Jackson, rock performer Jerry Lee Lewis, actress Reese Witherspoon, and pop singer Britney Spears.

Good food is important to Louisianans and is a large part of their culture. In fact, some of the state's biggest celebrities are chefs, such as Paul Prudhomme and Emeril Legasse. Dishes reflect the variety of people who lived in or came to Louisiana over the years. The American Indians contributed cornbread and a spice called filé to the Louisiana mix. Beignets, square donuts sprinkled with powdered sugar, were brought by the French. Spicy peppers from the Spanish added flavor to many Louisiana dishes.

Where Is Louisiana?

Louisiana's favorable location at the mouth of the Mississippi River, where it flows into the Gulf of Mexico, has made the area highly desirable property throughout its history. First inhabited by American Indians, Louisiana was explored by the Spanish in the 1500s and claimed by the French in 1682. For nearly four decades in the late 1700s, Spain ruled Louisiana, only to return it to France in 1800. The United States bought the land in the Louisiana Purchase of 1803, but the state's early history remains evident in the many French and Spanish names on its map. Louisiana also has a strong French and Spanish heritage in its population, customs, and architecture.

During the mid-1800s, Louisiana developed into a rich agricultural area. Fertile soil and slave labor allowed sugarcane and cotton **plantations** to flourish. In 1861, before the outbreak of the Civil War, Louisiana withdrew from the Union and joined the Confederate States of America. It was readmitted to the Union as a state in 1868 after drawing up a new constitution granting equal rights to its black population. For many years after the war, the economy struggled, but the state made progress in the 1900s with the development of its rich mineral resources and its manufacturing industries.

Most of Louisiana's cotton grows in the northeastern part of the state.

Although the Civil War ended slavery, **segregation** was legal in Louisiana, and a huge gap between African Americans and whites remained in income and education. As in much of the United States, the 1950s and 1960s saw the rise of the civil rights movement in Louisiana, and the educational and income gap began to narrow. During the 1990s, however, Louisiana was one of the poorest states in the nation, and by 2009, 17 percent of its population was considered to live in poverty.

On August 29, 2005, Hurricane Katrina struck the Gulf Coast, including Louisiana, Florida, Mississippi, and Alabama. It was the most destructive hurricane in U.S. history. More than 1,800 people were killed, 1,200 of them Louisianans. About 80 percent of New Orleans was covered with water when the **levees** protecting the city broke. Fundraising across the nation and the world brought resources to rebuild the city and outlying regions. However, half a dozen years later, the city and state had still not completely recovered from the damage from the storm.

Volunteer and paid construction workers continue to build new houses and repair damaged homes after Hurricane Katrina.

Mapping Louisiana

Louisiana lies in the part of the United States known as the Deep South. It shares its borders with Arkansas to the north, Mississippi to the east, and Texas to the west. To the south lies the Gulf of Mexico. With all the shipping on the Mississippi River and in the Gulf, Louisiana's southern coast is one of the busiest commercial areas in the country.

Sites and Symbols

STATE SEAL
Louisiana

STATE BIRD
Eastern Brown Pelican

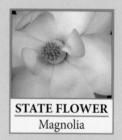

STATE FLOWER
Magnolia

STATE FLAG
Louisiana

STATE DOG
Catahoula Leopard Dog

STATE TREE
Bald Cypress

Nickname The Pelican State

Motto Union, Justice, Confidence

Song "Give Me Louisiana" by Doralise Fontane and "You Are My Sunshine" by Jimmie Davis

Entered the Union April 30, 1812, as the 18th state

Capital Baton Rouge

Population (2010 Census) 4,533,372 Ranked 25th state

ARKANSAS

MISSISSIPPI

Hooks
Texarkana
Magnolia
Hamburg
Starkville
Haynesville
Eudora
Durant
Homer
Bastrop
Yazoo City
Canton
Minden
Lake Providence
Bossier City
Ruston
20
Monroe
Delhi
Jackson
Forest
Meridian
Shreveport
Tallulah
Vicksburg
Pearl
Newton
Jonesboro
Quitman
Henderson
Mansfield
Port Gibson
Winnfield
Laurel
49
Natchitoches
Natchez
Brookhaven
59
Zwolle
LOUISIANA
Center
McComb
Hattiesburg
Nacogdoches
Many
Alexandria
Ball
Purvis
Fort Polk South
55
Amite City
Poplarville
Jasper
Bunkie
Kentwood
Picayune
De Ridder
49
New Roads
55
Orange Grove
Woodville
Opelousas
Baker
Hammond
12
Biloxi
TEXAS
Baton Rouge
12
Kountze
Lafayette
Gonzales
55
Slidell
Lumberton
Sulphur
Crowley
Baldwin
Kenner
Estelle
Beaumont
New Iberia
New Orleans
10
Abbeville
Morgan City
Port
Arthur
Houma
Port Sulphur
Galliano
Port Triumph

N

Map Scale

0   100 Miles

United States

Hawai'i   Alaska

Louisiana

STATE CAPITAL

Baton Rouge means "red post" in French. It was named by the explorer Pierre Le Moyne, who spotted a post made from a Louisiana red cypress tree that marked the boundary between two American Indian groups. Besides being a major U.S. **port**, Baton Rouge is a hub for the chemical and petroleum industries. The 34-story State Capitol is the city's tallest building.

The Land

Louisiana is a fertile lowland divided into three main areas. These regions are the East Gulf Coastal Plain, the Mississippi **Alluvial** Plain, and the West Gulf Coastal Plain.

Louisiana is known for its swamps and marshes. Its highest point, Driskill Mountain in the northwest, is only 535 feet above sea level. The city of New Orleans, the lowest point in the state, lies 5 feet below sea level.

More than 7,400 square miles of Louisiana are underwater. The low, wet land is excellent for raising crops, but it also floods easily. To keep the floodwaters from destroying homes and farmlands, long, high mounds called levees have been built throughout the state.

KISATCHIE NATIONAL FOREST

The Kisatchie National Forest covers more than 604,000 acres spread over seven **parishes**. Thick stands of pine trees tower overhead while wild orchids and grasses, such as toothache and panic, grow in shady or sunlit areas. Tupelos and bald cypress trees thrive in its swamps.

ATCHAFALAYA DELTA

The Atchafalaya Delta is part of the Mississippi Alluvial Plain. Large quantities of water from the Mississippi River flow into the delta. It is one of the few areas in Louisiana where the coastline is actually increasing, because of silt deposits from the river.

SWAMP

Cypress trees grow well in swamps, which are wetlands partially covered with water. There are many swamps in Louisiana's Alluvial Plain.

BAYOU

Small, slow-moving rivers, bayous wander through the wetlands along Louisiana's coast, splitting into many branches that flow in different directions.

While hurricanes are common in Louisiana, Hurricane Katrina in 2005 caused the most damage in the state's history. Water poured through the streets of New Orleans.

Climate

Louisiana's climate is humid in most areas, with mild winters and hot summers. The average temperature in the south rises from 55° Fahrenheit in January to 82° F in July. The average temperature in northern Louisiana ranges from 49° F in January to 82° F in July. Louisiana is one of the wettest states, receiving a yearly average of 48 inches of rainfall in the northeast and 66 inches in the southwest. New Orleans is one of the wettest major cities in the United States. Hurricanes from the Gulf of Mexico sometimes hit Louisiana.

The highest temperature ever recorded in Louisiana was 114° F on August 10, 1936, in Plain Dealing. At the other extreme, a record low reading of –16° F was recorded on February 13, 1899, in Minden.

Average Annual Precipitation Across Louisiana

Cities in different parts of Louisiana typically receive different amounts of rainfall over the course of a year. Why might New Orleans get the highest amount of precipitation?

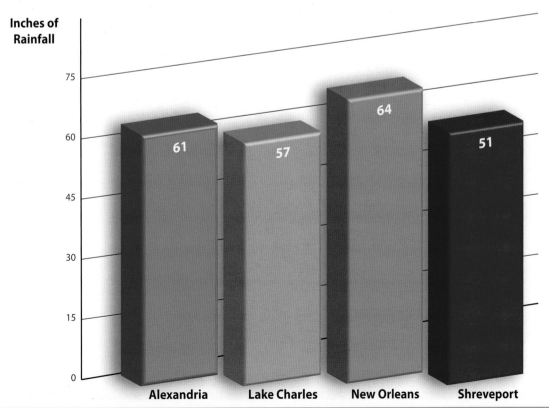

Inches of Rainfall

Alexandria	Lake Charles	New Orleans	Shreveport
61	57	64	51

Natural Resources

Before the discovery of oil in Louisiana, fishing, trapping animals for their fur, and farming were very important to the economy. As some small farms grew into large plantations during the late 1700s and early 1800s, crops such as sugarcane and cotton became vital.

Louisiana's woodlands support a profitable forestry industry. It supplies wood for pulp and paper mills, as well as pine plywood and lumber for construction.

When oil was discovered in 1901, the Louisiana economy changed. Oil drilling and refining became a major source of income. Large, federally controlled reserves are located off the Gulf Coast. The state also has significant reserves of natural gas, which is another important energy source.

Along with these fuel minerals, Louisiana has huge salt and sulfur resources. The salt deposits are contained in large underground formations, some of which are a mile across and almost 50,000 feet deep. Sulfur is an important mineral used in thousands of products and processes. The first sulfur mined in the United States came from Louisiana.

With nearly 14 million acres of forests, Louisiana is a major producer of lumber. Pine, oak, gum, and cypress trees are all harvested in the state.

Louisiana's mines produce salt for melting snow on roads and to put in food.

Plants

Woodland and prairie plants grow in some of the northern part of the state. In areas of central Louisiana, towering stands of pine trees cover land dotted with wild azaleas, sassafras trees, and blazing star flowers. Insect-eating plants include sundews, butterworts, and bright yellow pitcher plants. This fertile area once supported acres of **indigo** and tobacco plantations and then cotton fields.

The wetlands of southern Louisiana are a natural haven for plants. Sedge grass, rushes, and palmetto scrub thrive in the wet conditions. Spanish moss hangs from the branches of cypress and oak trees in swamps and marshes. This moss can be an eerie sight, resembling a long gray beard. The magnolia, whose blossom is the state flower, grows throughout the state.

Cypress swamps along Louisiana's coast protect the land from being washed away by hurricanes. They reduce the tidal surges, or huge waves, caused by the storms. They also slow hurricane wind speeds.

CYPRESS TREES

Cypress trees thrive in warm, wet climates. They can grow to heights of more than 80 feet. They shelter migrating birds and provide food to geese, ducks, and rabbits.

AZALEAS

Azaleas are low-growing, flowering bushes that prefer shaded areas. Their fragrant blossoms may be red, pink, purple, or white.

LOBLOLLY PINE

Loblolly pines produce a large number of cones every year that contain seeds, which birds and squirrels feed on.

IRIS

Irises have leaves that look like long swords. Their flowers can be blue, purple, yellow, pink, white, or dark red.

Louisiana has almost 1 million acres of wildlife refuge areas.

Magnolias were growing during the time of the dinosaurs.

At one time, citizens of Louisiana tried to designate the iris as the state flower and name the magnolia as the state tree, but they were unsuccessful. Mississippi also has the magnolia as its state flower.

A pitcher plant's leaves are shaped like tubes with a lid partially covering the top. Attracted by the plant's nectar, insects start to climb down the tube on stiff hairs. Then they reach a smooth area and slide down to the juices below that will digest them.

The leaves, bark, and roots of the sassafras tree can be made into flavorings, medicine, and tea. Root beer was once made from sassafras.

Animals

Louisiana has thousands of ponds and bayous that are home to bullfrogs, catfish, bass, and crayfish, which are called crawfish in the state. Alligators are also found in these lowland, watery areas. Muskrats and other fur-bearing rodents also live in the marshes.

Louisiana has many different kinds of birds, both native and **migrant**. The Eastern brown pelican is the state bird of Louisiana, but it is becoming a rare sight in the state. Its cousin, the white pelican, is far more common. Pelican nesting grounds are in the coastal marshes.

Forests cover almost one-half of Louisiana. These areas are inhabited by animals such as deer, otters, coyotes, rabbits, skunks, opossums, and gray foxes. Louisiana black bears were once found throughout the state, but now they are rare. They roam the forests of the Tensas and Atchafalaya River basins.

AMERICAN BLACK BEAR

Louisiana's black bears eat wild berries and acorns. They also graze on corn, wheat, oats, and sugarcane growing in farm fields. Black bears can weigh up to 600 pounds, and males are much larger than females.

FERAL PIG

While wild pigs may look like domestic pigs, their fur is much coarser and longer. Their varied diet includes roots, grasses, crayfish, and frogs.

NUTRIA

During the 1930s, nutrias were brought to Louisiana to be raised for their fur. They escaped into the marshes and have flourished there ever since. They feed on wetland plants and have damaged areas of southeastern Louisiana.

SNOWY EGRET

Egrets live in lakes, marshes, and coastal areas. About 2 feet tall, egrets hunt frogs, fish, reptiles, and mammals for food.

I DIDN'T KNOW THAT!

Many of the ducks and geese in North America spend their winters along the Louisiana coast.

The honeybee, which is the official state insect, does more than make delicious honey. Honeybees also pollinate crops and plants.

Louisiana's freshwater fish include bass, catfish, and sunfish. Tarpon and pompano are among the more unusual fish that live in the Gulf of Mexico.

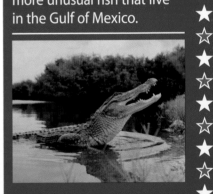

The state reptile is the American alligator. With almost no predators besides people, the species has survived since the time of the dinosaurs.

Southern Louisiana is the crayfish capital of the world. The crayfish industry brings in millions of dollars each year.

Tourism

Louisiana celebrates the annual Mardi Gras festival. The season traditionally begins on January 6 and lasts about two months. Massive celebrations, particularly in New Orleans and surrounding communities, occur in the final week of the carnival season, the week of Mardi Gras. Louisiana residents and tourists alike celebrate by wearing masks and colorful clothing and marching in street parades. The Mardi Gras festival draws tourists from around the world.

Many visitors also come to Louisiana to taste its world-famous cuisine. No trip is complete without sampling the flavors of Cajun and Creole dishes.

The old plantation mansions are another popular tourist attraction. Centuries ago, as plantation owners grew richer, their homes became quite elaborate. These estate owners tried to make their lives as elegant as possible by planting large gardens and beautifying their homes. Some estates are now open to the public. In some places, rows of mansions line leafy, tree-lined avenues.

FISHING

A chance to catch a wide variety of fish lures tourists to Louisiana. Speckled trout, flounder, black drum fish, sheepshead fish, and redfish all flourish in the state's saltwater bayous.

NEW ORLEANS

Tourists enjoy the Old World charm of New Orleans, which is known for its distinctive combination of Spanish and French architecture. Horse-drawn carriages can be hired to tour the beautiful French Quarter.

NEW ORLEANS JAZZ AND HERITAGE FESTIVAL

The New Orleans Jazz and Heritage Festival showcases musicians from all over Louisiana and the world. Listeners come to come to dance and hear jazz, Cajun, **zydeco**, pop, and rhythm and blues. Tourists and Louisianans alike flock for the food as well, including crawfish Monica, fried oyster and shrimp sandwiches, gumbo, and pecan pie.

AVERY ISLAND

Avery Island is home not only to salt mines but also to the McIlhenny Company, which makes the popular Tabasco sauce. This sauce, made with vinegar, red peppers, and Avery Island salt, is aged for up to three years in oak barrels.

I DIDN'T KNOW THAT!

Tourists spend a billion dollars in Louisiana every year in hotels, restaurants, stores, and other attractions.

Cajun meals are a combination of French and Southern cuisines. Cajun dishes include **jambalaya** and coush-coush, a thick cornmeal breakfast dish.

Creole food is a blend of French, Spanish, and African cuisines. One of the most famous Creole dishes is **gumbo**.

The plantation culture developed along the state's rivers and bayous, where planters first used the rich soil to raise indigo and tobacco. They later added to these crops, growing cotton in the north and sugarcane in the south.

Industry

The invention of the steam engine provided a major boost to Louisiana's economy. During the early 1800s, steam-powered riverboats began traveling the Mississippi River, transporting goods and people. By 1840, New Orleans was the second-largest port in the country. Today New Orleans is still an important port city. Ships bring in coffee, seafood, oil, and gas.

Industries in Louisiana
Value of Goods and Services in Millions of Dollars

Tourism is very important to the economy of Louisiana. What are some industries that might get a significant part of their income from meeting the needs of tourists?

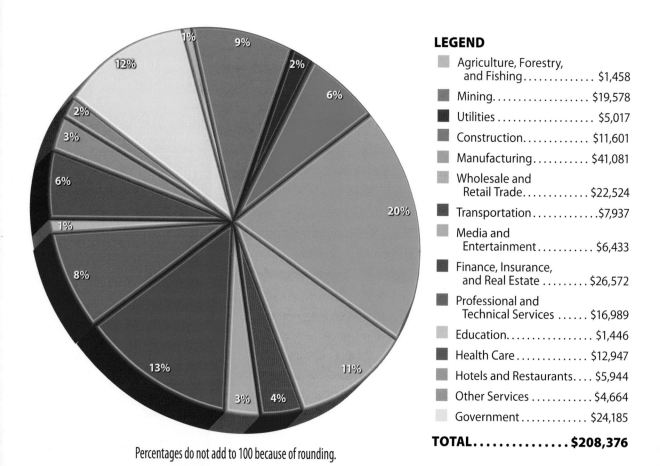

LEGEND

Industry	Value
Agriculture, Forestry, and Fishing	$1,458
Mining	$19,578
Utilities	$5,017
Construction	$11,601
Manufacturing	$41,081
Wholesale and Retail Trade	$22,524
Transportation	$7,937
Media and Entertainment	$6,433
Finance, Insurance, and Real Estate	$26,572
Professional and Technical Services	$16,989
Education	$1,446
Health Care	$12,947
Hotels and Restaurants	$5,944
Other Services	$4,664
Government	$24,185
TOTAL	**$208,376**

Percentages do not add to 100 because of rounding.

Oil drilling and refining is another major industry in Louisiana. The state is among the top five oil-producing states. Louisiana's oil refineries produce billions of gallons of gasoline each year. One oil refinery in Baton Rouge produces half a million barrels per day.

Fishing is also a valuable industry in Louisiana. The state is a leading producer of shrimps and oysters. Louisiana fishers catch crabs, red snapper, and tuna as well.

To help industries grow in the state, the government of Louisiana is encouraging people to start small businesses by making rules and regulations more flexible. It has also created a workforce-training program to assist new businesses in finding trained workers.

Every year, Louisiana petroleum refineries produce enough gasoline to fill 800 million automobile gas tanks.

Oil companies first developed techniques for offshore oil drilling off the Louisiana coast.

The state's fishing industry accounts for about one-fourth of all the seafood caught in the United States.

Louisiana is the largest handler of grain for export in the country.

The Louisiana Offshore Oil Port (LOOP), in the Gulf of Mexico about 20 miles southeast of Port Fourchon, is one of the few U.S. ports able to receive extremely large oil tankers. It is sometimes called the Superport.

Besides gasoline, Louisiana refineries also produce jet fuels and hundreds of other petroleum products.

Goods and Services

Louisiana's oil and natural gas reserves are the source of many products besides gasoline and other fuels. The state's large petrochemical industry makes chemicals from oil and natural gas. These chemicals are used for a variety of commercial purposes. Valuable petrochemical products made in Louisiana include plastics and fertilizers. Petrochemicals are also used in making soaps and detergents, paints, medicines, cosmetics, and many other goods.

Shipyards in Louisiana construct oil tankers as well as combat ships for the U.S. Navy.

New Orleans is one of the three main ports in the United States for receiving coffee beans from around the world. A New Orleans specialty coffee is made from roasted coffee beans and roasted ground chicory root.

Apart from oil and chemicals, Louisiana's factories also manufacture hundreds of other products. They include telephone systems, light trucks, electrical equipment, glass products, automobile batteries, mobile homes, playground equipment, and clothing. The state is also known for producing transportation equipment such as ships, truck trailers, and aircraft.

Food processing is also important to the economy. Louisiana factories produce such foods as coffee, sugar, and soft drinks. Coffee beans brought in from Latin America are processed in New Orleans. Many of the state's larger cities have soft-drink bottling factories. Sugar refineries are also prominent in Louisiana.

Louisiana is among the country's leading producers of sweet potatoes, rice, sugarcane, cotton, and pecans.

Cotton has long been a leading crop in Louisiana. There is a cotton museum in Lake Providence.

Louisiana has historically been a leading fur-producing state. Nutrias, muskrats, mink, and raccoons are all fur sources.

The first charity hospital in the United States was in Louisiana.

Louisiana plants built the huge Saturn C-5 rocket boosters used in the Apollo space program that sent astronauts to the moon.

Many chemicals are manufactured in Baton Rouge, New Orleans, and Shreveport.

Paper mills in northern Louisiana produce a great variety of paper products.

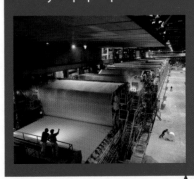

American Indians

American Indians lived on the land that is now Louisiana for thousands of years before European explorers arrived. Evidence of an Indian civilization dating from about 700 BC has been uncovered at a place now called Poverty Point. However, most of what we know today about Louisiana's native peoples is based on the records of European explorers who began arriving in the 1500s and 1600s. The largest American Indian group in the area was the Caddo, who lived in the northwest. The explorers also encountered the Natchez, who lived in the middle of the state, the Atakapas in the southeast, the Chitimachans in the south, Muskogeans in the east, and the Tunicans in the northeast, among others. These groups spoke different languages and had different cultures.

The Mound Builder culture flourished in Louisiana almost 3,000 years ago. These Indians built huge mounds to contain and honor their dead and to serve as temples. Emerald Mound is the second-largest temple mound in the United States.

The American Indians of Louisiana grew many different crops, including corn, pumpkins, squash, melons, and beans. They also gathered wild nuts and fruits, hunted game with blowguns and arrows, and set woven nets across streams to catch fish.

The meeting of Europeans and American Indians often had disastrous results. Although the Europeans had the advantage of guns, the most dangerous weapon they carried with them was disease. Indians had never been exposed to many European illnesses and so had poor **immunity** to them. Many American Indians died after being exposed to diseases such as smallpox, measles, and tuberculosis.

Natchez men dressed in leggings and breechcloths made of deerskin while the women wore skirts or dresses of woven fibers. In the winter, they added a robe.

When Europeans began to settle the area that became Louisiana in the early 1700s, perhaps as many as 12,000 American Indians from some 30 tribes were already living there.

Other tribes moved to Louisiana during the late 1700s and early 1800s, including the Alabamas and the Quapaws. Both were moved to Indian reservations in Texas and Oklahoma by the mid-1800s.

The Caddos mined salt, which they traded to other American Indian tribes.

The Chitimacha are the only Indian tribe in Louisiana to have kept some of their ancient lands.

The Choctaws played a game called *ishtaboli* with two teams. Each team had up to 100 players. Each player used two rackets to try to hit a leather ball into the opposing team's goal.

The Natchez were organized into four different social classes. They ranged in order from lowest to highest as the Stinkards, the Honored Men, the Nobles, and the Suns. The upper classes had to marry individuals from the lower classes.

Explorers

The king of Spain arranged for the first organized exploration by Europeans of the land that became Louisiana. He had heard stories of a river in the New World that was a rich source of gold. With this wealth in mind, he sent explorer Hernando de Soto to find the river. In 1541, de Soto reached the Mississippi River at what is now Memphis, Tennessee. He and his men followed the river south, but de Soto died before they reached the mouth of the river, at the Gulf of Mexico. Still, his men were likely the first Europeans to set foot on Louisiana soil.

The adventurous René-Robert Cavelier, sieur de La Salle, arrived in Canada from France in the 1660s. In 1682, he set out by boat down the Mississippi River with a group of fellow explorers. After a dangerous journey, La Salle's group arrived at the mouth of the Mississippi. La Salle planted a wooden cross bearing the French coat of arms and claimed the entire Mississippi Valley for France. He ignored the American Indians' previous claim to the land.

Hernando de Soto came to Louisiana in an unsuccessful search for gold and other riches.

Timeline of Settlement

Early Exploration

1519 Álvarez de Pineda leads an expedition along the Gulf Coast and explores the mouth of the Mississippi River.

1541–1542 Hernando de Soto explores the Mississippi River south of present-day Memphis.

1682 René-Robert Cavalier, sieur de La Salle, claims a huge territory, including what is now the state of Louisiana, for King Louis XIV of France. The region becomes known as the Louisiana Territory.

Early European Settlements

1715 Louis Juchereau de St. Denis establishes Fort St. Jean Baptiste, the first permanent settlement in the Mississippi Valley.

1718 Jean-Baptiste Le Moyne, sieur de Bienville, founds New Orleans, named for Philippe II, duc d'Orléans.

1762 Louis XV gives the Louisiana Territory west of the Mississippi River to his cousin, King Charles III of Spain.

1763 France gives the Florida Parishes, on the border of present-day Mississippi, to Great Britain.

Louisiana Joins the United States

1803 Three years after Spain returns the Louisiana Territory to France, the United States, under the leadership of President Thomas Jefferson, purchases the territory from Emperor Napoleon I of France for $15 million.

1804 Louisiana is divided into the Territory of New Orleans and the District of Louisiana.

Statehood and Civil War

1812 Louisiana is admitted to the Union as the 18th state.

1861 Louisiana secedes from, or leaves, the Union and joins the Confederacy at the beginning of the Civil War.

1868 Three years after the Confederacy is defeated at the end of the Civil War, Louisiana is readmitted to the Union as a state.

Early Settlers

King Louis XIV sent Pierre Le Moyne, sieur d'Iberville, to the mouth of the Mississippi River to build a colony. Iberville arrived in 1699 and established a settlement on Biloxi Bay. The following year, he built a second settlement near the site of present-day New Orleans.

Map of Settlements and Resources in Early Louisiana

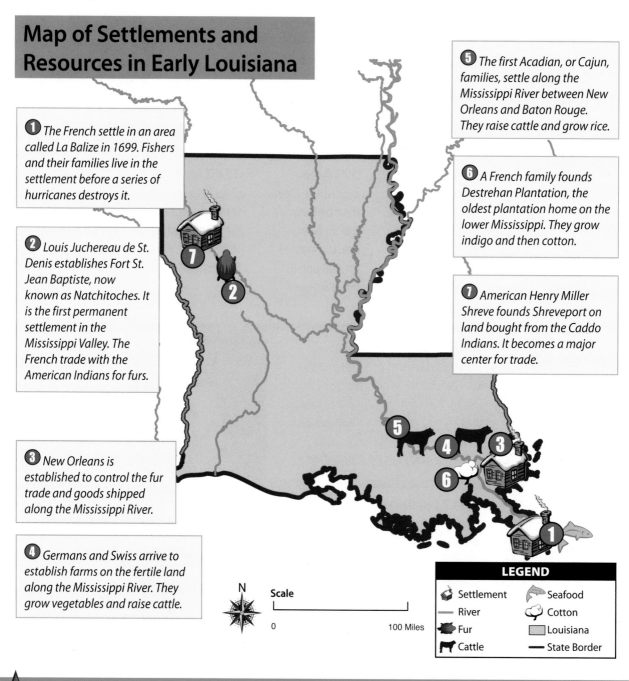

1 The French settle in an area called La Balize in 1699. Fishers and their families live in the settlement before a series of hurricanes destroys it.

2 Louis Juchereau de St. Denis establishes Fort St. Jean Baptiste, now known as Natchitoches. It is the first permanent settlement in the Mississippi Valley. The French trade with the American Indians for furs.

3 New Orleans is established to control the fur trade and goods shipped along the Mississippi River.

4 Germans and Swiss arrive to establish farms on the fertile land along the Mississippi River. They grow vegetables and raise cattle.

5 The first Acadian, or Cajun, families, settle along the Mississippi River between New Orleans and Baton Rouge. They raise cattle and grow rice.

6 A French family founds Destrehan Plantation, the oldest plantation home on the lower Mississippi. They grow indigo and then cotton.

7 American Henry Miller Shreve founds Shreveport on land bought from the Caddo Indians. It becomes a major center for trade.

N

Scale

0   100 Miles

LEGEND

Settlement		Seafood	
River		Cotton	
Fur		Louisiana	
Cattle		State Border	

In 1718, Pierre's brother, Jean Baptiste Le Moyne, sieur de Bienville, chose a spot south of Lake Ponchartrain for a new settlement, which he named Nouvelle Orleans, now called New Orleans.

Colonization increased during the 1760s with the arrival of the French-speaking Acadians, who had been forced from Canada by the British. The Acadians became known as Cajuns.

In 1762, France turned the Louisiana region over to Spain. Spain returned Louisiana to France in 1800.

In the early 1800s, the United States wanted new territory to increase its western frontier. President Thomas Jefferson sent American representatives to France to meet with the emperor Napoleon and negotiate the purchase of the Louisiana Territory. Under a treaty signed in 1803, the residents of Louisiana went from being French to being American in the deal that became known as the Louisiana Purchase.

Jean Baptiste Le Moyne served as governor of the French colony for a number of years and laid out the boundaries of New Orleans.

I DIDN'T KNOW THAT!

Jean Baptiste Le Moyne, sieur de Bienville, made New Orleans the capital of Louisiana in 1722.

The Louisiana Purchase of 1803 was one of the best real estate bargains in history. For only $15 million, the United States acquired about 828,000 square miles of land, doubling the size of the country. That amount averages to about three cents per acre of land.

The oldest cathedral in the United States, the St. Louis Cathedral in New Orleans, was built in 1718.

A year after President Jefferson oversaw the Louisiana Purchase, he sent Meriwether Lewis and William Clark on an expedition to explore the area.

Notable People

While the people of Louisiana are well-known for their music and their food, there is much more to their history. They have been Civil War heroes, activists, designers, politicians, doctors, and much more. Many notable Louisianans have contributed to their state and the world.

PIERRE GUSTAVE TOUTANT (P.G.T.) BEAUREGARD (1818–1893)

Born in St. Bernard Parish, Beauregard was raised on a sugar plantation. After attending the U.S. Military Academy at West Point, he served in the Mexican-American War. In 1861, when the Civil War began, he left the U.S. military to join the Confederate Army. Beauregard led the attack against Fort Sumter, the first battle in the Civil War. With this attack and his victory at the Battle of Bull Run, he became a hero to the South.

MADAME C.J. WALKER (1867–1919)

Her slave parents named her Sarah Breedlove when she was born in Delta. In 1905, she created a hair care formula for African American women. She built a financial empire out of this product and others. When she married Charles Walker in 1906, she began calling herself Madame C.J. Walker. The first female African American millionaire, she was known for her generosity and gave to campaigns against lynching and to support the rights of African Americans.

HUEY P. LONG (1893–1935)

Born to a farming family, Huey Long became a popular but controversial governor after his election in 1928. His programs provided free textbooks to schoolchildren, built about 13,000 miles of roads, increased the number of state hospitals for the poor, and funded improvements in the port of New Orleans. The public was less supportive when he tried to get rid of the state poll tax in order to make it easier for blacks and poor whites to vote.

GEOFFREY BEENE (1927–2004)

Beene grew up in Haynesville in a family of doctors. He quickly abandoned his medical school training to focus on designing women's fashion. His work featured fluid designs and unusual fabrics, creating an original look with crisp lines. His fashions continue to inspire young designers.

ANDREW YOUNG (1932–)

Young became the first African American to serve as U.S. ambassador to the United Nations. He was born in New Orleans and became a prominent member of the civil rights movement. He was jailed for taking part in civil rights protests. Young was elected mayor of Atlanta, Georgia, in 1982.

I DIDN'T KNOW THAT!

Michael DeBakey (1908–2008) is well-known for his work on the human heart. DeBakey, along with another surgeon, successfully implanted the first assisting heart. This machine is inserted into the chest and helps a weak heart pump blood until a transplant is available or the heart recovers. He also developed artificial blood vessels. He was born in Lake Charles, Louisiana.

Lindy Boggs (1916–) served in the U.S. House of Representatives for 18 years, starting in 1973. She was the first woman from Louisiana elected to Congress. She also served as ambassador to the Vatican. As chair of the 1976 Democratic National Convention, she was the first woman to preside over a major political party convention.

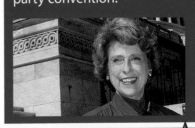

Population

The people of Louisiana are a mix of ethnic groups and cultures. According to Census Bureau estimates, nearly 65 percent of the state's population is white, and 32 percent is African American. In comparison, the national population is about 80 percent white and 13 percent black. The state's population also includes small percentages of Asian Americans and American Indians. About 4 percent of the people of Louisiana are Hispanic Americans, and about 3 percent of Louisianians were born in another country.

Louisiana Population 1950–2010

The population of Louisiana grew by only a little more than one percent between 2000 and 2010. How did Hurricane Katrina affect the state's rate of population growth?

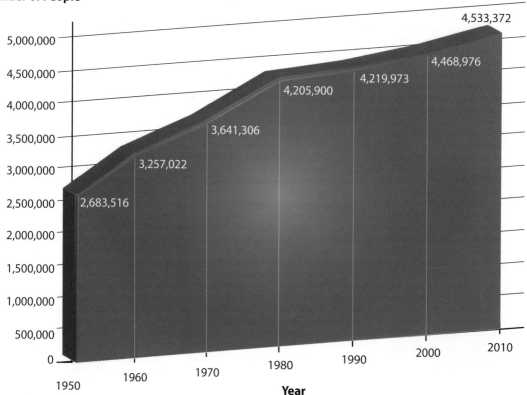

Number of People

- 1950: 2,683,516
- 1960: 3,257,022
- 1970: 3,641,306
- 1980: 4,205,900
- 1990: 4,219,973
- 2000: 4,468,976
- 2010: 4,533,372

Year

Slightly less than 75 percent of the people of Louisiana have graduated from high school, compared to 80 percent of all the people in the United States. Nearly 19 percent of Louisianans have graduated from college, while 24 percent of all Americans have a bachelor's college degree or higher.

The majority of Louisiana's people lived in rural areas until 1950, but the number of city dwellers grew rapidly after that. By the start of the 21st century, nearly three-fourths of Louisiana's population lived in urban areas. New Orleans is the largest city, followed by the capital, Baton Rouge, which is also the center of the chemical industry. Other population centers are Lafayette in south-central Louisiana and Shreveport in the northwest. Northern and western Louisiana are much less populated than the southern end of the state.

I DIDN'T KNOW THAT!

New Orleans' population dropped dramatically after Hurricane Katrina struck in 2005, but it has started increasing again. The New Orleans metropolitan area now has more than 1,190,000 residents, about 90 percent of its pre-Katrina population.

In 2009, African Americans made up about 61 percent of the residents of New Orleans.

Baton Rouge, the second largest city in Louisiana, has almost 230,000 people, followed by Shreveport, with about 200,000 people.

Shreveport lies on the Red River and is home to hundreds of manufacturing plants. A convention center, a performing arts center, and a garden and art center line its riverfront.

Politics and Government

When Louisiana entered the Union in 1812, it brought with it a system of law that came from France. The system still exists today, though every other state in the nation follows the English common law system. The main difference between the two types of law is that judges in Louisiana rely more on a system of written laws, while judges in other states are more influenced by decisions made in earlier cases.

The Louisiana State Capitol building houses the Louisiana state legislature, the governor's office, and parts of the executive branch.

When Bobby Jindal took office as governor of Louisiana in 2008, he became the first Indian American to be chosen as the chief executive of any state.

Louisiana has two state songs.

Here is an excerpt from the song "Give Me Louisiana."

*Give me Louisiana,
The State where I was born
The State of snowy cotton,
The best I've ever known;
A State of sweet magnolias,
And Creole melodies.*

Here's an excerpt from the song "You Are My Sunshine."

*You Are My Sunshine
My only sunshine.
You make me happy
When skies are grey.
You'll never know, dear,
How much I love you.
Please don't take my
  sunshine away.*

Another leftover from the days of French and Spanish rule is the political division of the state. Rather than counties, Louisiana is divided into 64 parishes, which were once managed by the Catholic church. Today most parishes are governed by a body called the police jury. No other state has this parish system.

Louisiana's governor is elected to a term of four years and cannot serve more than two terms in a row. The head of state government, the governor also appoints many members of state agencies, boards, and commissions. The legislature passes laws. Louisiana's legislature is made up of two parts. The Senate has 39 members, and the House of Representatives has 105 members. Each member is elected to a four-year term.

The Supreme Court is the highest court in the state. Each of its seven justices is elected for a ten-year term. Judges in the lower courts are also usually elected rather than appointed.

Cultural Groups

At the time of the Louisiana Purchase, Louisiana's culture was far more French than American. Many of the first settlers in the area had come from France and from areas in Canada settled by the French. Spanish traders also arrived. The descendants of these early settlers were known as Creoles, a term that originally meant "native of the colony." Today the word means different things to different people. It can refer to a variety of combinations of French, Spanish, African, Caribbean, and American Indian cultures. Among Louisiana's Creoles, though, the French influence is especially strong.

Traditional Creole culture lives on in the state. Natchitoches Parish in northwestern Louisiana celebrates the history and culture of the area's Creole community. Cane River National Heritage Area, preserves several plantations from the 1800s and other historic sites associated with Creole culture.

In New Orleans, African Americans hold parades during Mardi Gras and throughout the year. Brass bands, dancers, and brightly dressed participants are all part of these events.

Cajun tradition lives on in Mamou. During the annual Cajun Courir de Mardi Gras, people chase chickens to make gumbo.

The Cajuns are another important cultural group in Louisiana. In 1755, British soldiers drove 15,000 French colonists from the eastern part of Canada now known as Nova Scotia. These settlers had named that land Acadia. Eventually about 4,000 Acadians settled in south-central Louisiana, bringing their French culture with them. Today descendants of these people are known as Cajuns. They speak a unique language that combines French with terms taken from their English, Spanish, German, American Indian, and black neighbors.

A trip through Cajun Country, as much of southern Louisiana is sometimes called, provides a glimpse into the Cajun culture. Each May, the town of Breaux Bridge hosts the Crawfish Festival, featuring crawfish races, the crowning of a Crawfish King and Queen, and Cajun music and dancing.

Since Louisiana's early days, African Americans have played an important role in its culture. In Lake Charles, the annual Black Heritage Festival offers gospel and zydeco music, art exhibits, and dance competitions. The Let the Good Times Roll Festival, held each year in Shreveport, also features black music, art, and cuisine.

Arts and Entertainment

More than perhaps anything else, Louisiana is known for Mardi Gras, a festival brought to Louisiana by the French. In English, its name means "Fat Tuesday." For many Christians, the next day is Ash Wednesday, which begins a period of fasting or self-denial. Mardi Gras is a time of celebration before this solemn period.

The Mardi Gras season begins with a series of parties across the state in January. New Orleans has the biggest Mardi Gras event of all. For nearly two months every year, peaking sometime in March, the city comes alive with music, dancing, colorful street parades, costumes, and floats. More than 1 million visitors enjoy the wild celebration.

Although the exact history is not clear, jazz is often said to have originated in New Orleans before moving up the Mississippi River to Memphis, St. Louis, and Chicago. The early New Orleans sound goes back to tribal African drumbeats and European classical music. It has also been influenced by blues and gospel music.

Colorful Mardi Gras outfits are often handmade and handed down for generations.

The Marsalis family is one of New Orleans' leading families of jazz artists. Ellis Marsalis, the father, has taught generations of jazz musicians.

Folklore has it that a New Orleans barber named Buddy Bolden picked up his cornet and blew the first notes of jazz. This new musical form quickly became famous in the Storyville neighborhood of New Orleans. Since then, the jazz sound has been played all over the world, though many of the top jazz musicians have come from Louisiana.

A very different form of music found only in Louisiana is that of the Cajuns. A Cajun band is made up of musicians who play fiddle, guitar, push-button accordion, and a set of steel triangles. The tunes are lively and usually sung in French. Almost every song is fast-paced and written with dancing in mind.

Zydeco is a newer style of music, growing out of the Creole musical tradition called La La. It also uses the push-button accordion, as well as a **washboard** and spoons.

Rosie Ledet writes and sings some of her zydeco songs in Creole French.

Sports

The New Orleans Saints of the National Football League and the New Orleans Hornets of the National Basketball Association are Louisiana's major professional sports teams. Led by star quarterback Drew Brees, the Saints won their first Super Bowl in 2010. Brees tied a Super Bowl record by completing 32 passes and was named the game's Most Valuable Player.

Although the 2010 Super Bowl was played elsewhere, the Saints' home field is the stadium that has hosted more Super Bowls than any other. The Louisiana Superdome, which opened in 1975, was the site of the championship game in 1978, 1981, 1986, 1990, 1997, and 2002. The Super Bowl is scheduled to return to New Orleans in 2013.

Since he arrived in New Orleans in 2005, Drew Brees has won the hearts of Louisianans not just with his outstanding play but with his praise and support of the city.

Another major football event that takes place in the Superdome is the annual postseason college football game called the Sugar Bowl. First played in 1935 at Tulane University in New Orleans, the game was moved to the Superdome in 1976. In 1998, the Sugar Bowl became part of the Bowl Championship Series. This series crowns the national champion of college football each year.

Football at the college level has long been an important part of Louisiana's sporting life. The Tigers of Louisiana State University have been competing for more than 100 years, appearing in the Sugar Bowl many times. Another well-known football team is found at Grambling State University in northern Louisiana. That team is also called the Tigers.

Born in Summerfield, Karl Malone played college basketball at Louisiana Tech. He went on to be one of the greatest players in the history of the National Basketball Association, scoring more than 36,000 points in a career that spanned 19 years.

I DIDN'T KNOW THAT!

The Superdome is used for a lot more than football. It has hosted rock concerts, political conventions, and even the pope.

When the Superdome opened in 1975, it was promoted as "a triumph of imagination."

The longest boxing match in history is thought to have been held in New Orleans in April 1893. It lasted 110 rounds, which took seven hours and 19 minutes. The match ended in a tie.

The Sugar Bowl is held every year on or around New Year's Day.

The New Orleans Saints received their nickname partly because the NFL awarded the team to New Orleans on All Saints Day, November 1, 1996. Another reason is that the song "When the Saints Go Marching In" is an unofficial theme song of New Orleans.

National Averages Comparison

The United States is a federal republic, consisting of fifty states and the District of Columbia. Alaska and Hawai'i are the only non-contiguous, or non-touching, states in the nation. Today, the United States of America is the third-largest country in the world in population. The United States Census Bureau takes a census, or count of all the people, every ten years. It also regularly collects other kinds of data about the population and the economy. How does Louisiana compare with the national average?

Comparison Chart

United States 2010 Census Data *	USA	Louisiana
Admission to Union	NA	April 30, 1812
Land Area (in square miles)	3,537,438.44	43,561.85
Population Total	308,745,538	4,533,372
Population Density (people per square mile)	87.28	104.07
Population Percentage Change (April 1, 2000, to April 1, 2010)	9.7%	1.4%
White Persons (percent)	72.4%	62.6%
Black Persons (percent)	12.6%	32.0%
American Indian and Alaska Native Persons (percent)	0.9%	0.7%
Asian Persons (percent)	4.8%	1.5%
Native Hawaiian and Other Pacific Islander Persons (percent)	0.2%	—
Some Other Race (percent)	6.2%	1.5%
Persons Reporting Two or More Races (percent)	2.9%	1.6%
Persons of Hispanic or Latino Origin (percent)	16.3%	4.2%
Not of Hispanic or Latino Origin (percent)	83.7%	95.8%
Median Household Income	$52,029	$43,635
Percentage of People Age 25 or Over Who Have Graduated from High School	80.4%	74.8%

*All figures are based on the 2010 United States Census, with the exception of the last two items. Percentages may not add to 100 because of rounding.

How to Improve My Community

Strong communities make strong states. Think about what features are important in your community. What do you value? Education? Health? Forests? Safety? Beautiful spaces? Government works to help citizens create ideal living conditions that are fair to all by providing services in communities. Consider what changes you could make in your community. How would they improve your state as a whole? Using this concept web as a guide, write a report that outlines the features you think are most important in your community and what improvements could be made. A strong state needs strong communities.

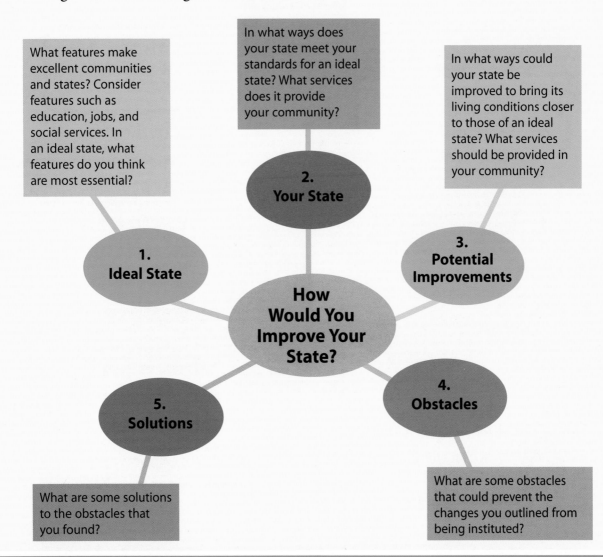

What features make excellent communities and states? Consider features such as education, jobs, and social services. In an ideal state, what features do you think are most essential?

In what ways does your state meet your standards for an ideal state? What services does it provide your community?

In what ways could your state be improved to bring its living conditions closer to those of an ideal state? What services should be provided in your community?

2. Your State

1. Ideal State

3. Potential Improvements

How Would You Improve Your State?

5. Solutions

4. Obstacles

What are some solutions to the obstacles that you found?

What are some obstacles that could prevent the changes you outlined from being instituted?

Exercise Your Mind!

Think about these questions and then use your research skills to find the answers and learn more fascinating facts about Louisiana. A teacher, librarian, or parent may be able to help you locate the best sources to use in your research.

5 Why is there a pelican on the flag of Louisiana?

1 Why is New Orleans sometimes called the Crescent City?

6 What is the most important product of Louisiana's fishing industry?

2 When did the United States purchase Louisiana from Napoleon, the French emperor?

7 These three Louisiana explorers are known by other names. What are they?

a) René-Robert Cavelier
b) Pierre Le Moyne
c) Jean Baptiste Le Moyne

3 What does Tabasco® sauce have to do with Louisiana?

8 What am I? My name means "Fat Tuesday" in French. Most people think of me as a party that lasts for several months. I take place in New Orleans every year.

4 What is the ethnic background of the Cajuns?

Words to Know

allegiance: loyalty or obedience to a country, ruler, or cause

alluvial: describing clay, silt, sand or gravel deposited by running water

gumbo: a type of soup or stew thickened by adding the vegetable okra

immunity: natural defenses

indigo: a plant that is used to make blue dye

jambalaya: a spicy Cajun dish

jazz: a form of music and dance that started in Louisiana, with African American origins

levees: either natural or artificial embankments built up beside a river to prevent flooding

migrant: moving from place to place with the seasons

parishes: districts, originally formed by a church and its leaders, that have become political districts in Louisiana

plantation: a large farm that is often worked by large number of people who live on the land

port: a place where ships dock in a harbor

segregation: the forced separation of races and restrictions based on race

washboard: a rippled board of metal, on which people scrub clothes, that is also used as a musical instrument

zydeco: a type of music with Cajun origins, played largely with fiddles, accordions, washboards, and spoons

Index

Log on to www.av2books.com

AV² by Weigl brings you media enhanced books that support active learning. Go to www.av2books.com, and enter the special code found on page 2 of this book. You will gain access to enriched and enhanced content that supplements and complements this book. Content includes video, audio, web links, quizzes, a slide show, and activities.

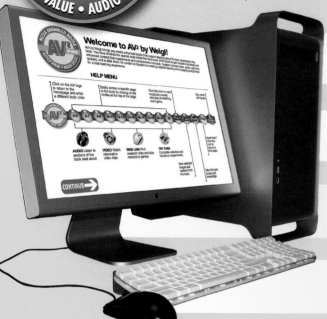

Audio
Listen to sections of the book read aloud.

Video
Watch informative video clips.

Embedded Weblinks
Gain additional information for research.

Try This!
Complete activities and hands-on experiments.

WHAT'S ONLINE?

Try This!	**Embedded Weblinks**	**Video**	**EXTRA FEATURES**
Test your knowledge of the state in a mapping activity.	Discover more attractions in Louisiana.	Watch a video introduction to Louisiana.	
Find out more about precipitation in your city.	Learn more about the history of the state.	Watch a video about the features of the state.	**Audio** Listen to sections of the book read aloud.
Plan what attractions you would like to visit in the state.	Learn the full lyrics of the state song.		**Key Words** Study vocabulary, and complete a matching word activity.
Learn more about the early natural resources of the state.			**Slide Show** View images and captions, and prepare a presentation.
Write a biography about a notable resident of Louisiana.			**Quizzes** Test your knowledge.
Complete an educational census activity.			

AV² was built to bridge the gap between print and digital. We encourage you to tell us what you like and what you want to see in the future.

Sign up to be an AV² Ambassador at www.av2books.com/ambassador.